LITTLE EASE

AHSAHTA PRESS

The New Series

NUMBER 15

LITTLE EASE

AARON McCOLLOUGH

AHSAHTA PRESS

BOISE STATE UNIVERSITY · BOISE · IDAHO · 2006

Ahsahta Press, Boise State University
Boise, Idaho 83725
http://ahsahtapress.boisestate.edu

Copyright © 2006 by Aaron McCollough
Printed in the United States of America
Cover design by Quemadura
Book design by Janet Holmes
First printing September 2006
ISBN-13: 978-0-916272-90-6

Library of Congress Cataloging-in-Publication Data

McCollough, Aaron.
    Little ease : poems / Aaron McCollough.
        p. cm. -- (The new series ; #15)
    ISBN-13: 978-0-916272-90-6 (pbk. : alk. paper)
    I. Title. II. Series: New series (Ahsahta Press) ; no. 15.

PS3613.C37L57 2006
811'.6--dc22
                                    2006005231

ACKNOWLEDGMENTS

Poems from this manuscript have appeared in *The Canary, Castagraf, The Colorado Review, Conduit, Denver Quarterly, Drunken Boat, Fence, LIT, Mantis, The New Review, Phoebe, Stride* (UK), *the tiny, Typo,* and *Verse*. Special thanks to Michael Schoenfeldt and Celeste Brusati. Thanks to Janet Holmes and everyone at Ahsahta Press: tireless and fearless.

FOR SUZANNE

"bereave me not,

Whereon I live, thy gentle looks, thy aid,
Thy counsel in this uttermost distress,
My onely strength and stay: forlorn of thee,
Whither shall I betake me, where subsist?"

– Milton, *Paradise Lost,* 10.918–922

CONTENTS

PROLOGUES FROM THE REFORMATIONS

SUPERLIMINARE

HOSPITALITY

SONNETS MANQUÉS

FROM THE RESTORATION   57

PENALTY

"A 'soul' inhabits him and brings him to existence, which is itself a factor in the mastery that power exercises over the body. The soul is the effect and instrument of a political anatomy; the soul is the prison of the body."

—Michel Foucault

"Thy God was making hast into thy roofe,
   Thy humble faith and feare keeps him aloofe:
Hee'l be thy Guest, because he may not be,
   Hee'l come—into thy house? no, into thee."

—Richard Crashaw

PROLOGUES FROM THE REFORMATIONS

first

Learning [I'm working the skin of the fruit with my thumbs until the entire surface] vanquishes nothing [in strips] beyond the illusion of the container. Consider the perspective box of Samuel Van Hoogstraten [darkens] where the painted light falls and where the painted shadow crouches and what do you consider? The reflection on the table through the door that isn't there [until the entire surface in strips darkens so there are no strips but only one dark print]. My friend calls it "the self as eye" – this trompe l'oeil she studies [in the cell that changes first].

second

We miniaturize. Call it the mobile eye coming in like light through a pinhole, free to flit from spectacle [dread samson brooding] to spectacle [over all Europe lurks the specter]. Cloistered [I'm winding the wire around the neg. pole] we learn we see only shadows then learn [around the pos. pole] to venture in shadow. How $58 \times 88 \times 63.5$ cm contains the restless soul. Mine, thine.—*'This dog is mine,' said those poor children; 'that is my place in the sun.' Here is the beginning and the image of the usurpation of all the earth.*

third

Experiment [with the tub drain gummed we're showering in gritty puddles] meaning *to see for yourself* meaning [with guests expected] imagine the tool, fashion the tool [we mix the box of soda with the jug of vinegar]. Remaining questions include if it works, how does it work [so the stuff erupts!]. How prove [the film cement]. Why prove [bright filament]. Prove why. Prove how   how prove how for why.

fourth

This work justifies [looking at the salad of the lawn] longing for rest [but thought will not permit] in constant spinning rest [the kind of work it takes to rest enough on grass to see in it] heuristic: the rest is vanity [the leaf that rustles with the leaves] at rest in needful vanity [the rest of the leaves] on earth [can we invite a god and bar] brutality's familiar, comfort [the world] which also moves with rest.

I

SUPERLIMINARE

the man is tying the woman's shoe

in the street

who smiles   at that

the household gods

I'm walking home today   hello   you

look so happy

                    yes, it's nice

nice   and how it colors all these faces

for now   from here

          is a

          shaped

          christmas in the universe

in September

native to this system

    o   nativity

as tree   is climbing

       lack and lackless sky

so terrifying

       out of

afraid like my animal

my heart   darting

around in the cavity of my body

should you see it

(the seal on the country of souls)

you'll know like the shambles

the inspectors are vague

to auditor   emperor   father   hovering
in aether (which knocks you out now)
(now whistles with signals)

we never can rest
   except always
we always can fly
   except

terror and love are my own
   I unleash them

&

the figure study   hampered

glossed in spirits of artichoke

craning tables with mug on its

peoples   every darling

          a birdman

cranky saint

saint with hand on crank

charge the well   wage the world

like pully   (through-tenon)

this ~~radial~~ steel-belted radial

two to radiant

          compose deeds as you

would have those who trespass

front-wheel-drive

      compose those who tresxpass

as you   Zuk: a test of poetry

no trigger

      doctor, explodeyerself

as long as the cooling in wide-spring   salt having /*cave*/ on the cavity in
the morning of this 200th day of my 31st; dreamt as this is the autumn
of the people's calendar   they, crying out the banners, drive the slick
roads beside me – the muskrat median sinking to these beriberi roots
(or) this classical hell (cavernous and candlelit, a place reserved for me
and my friends). I may return from lunch for lunch snarfed on the run
to tasks cleaning the universe of stables of the university. I may rage
against the hour hand s/he rules with a shot-glass of shavings   and kiss
my good wife before incredible journeys

we swim in underwear
  @ roadside lodges
screwing salt into the threads
  for what we come to
knows us by
  and by
the rotting railings
  raining in the future
our birds are bathing
o draw   a   bath   my dear
  dra   b   y ear
o r   d ar   ing
    inin in
  e ro   s
        hat   e   me
    wing s   to
t   e lo   s
        im in   we

&

@ the funeral home

kentucky plates
            a kentuckian

is dying

    whose politics are

banal as well

    as   I am like my marriage

which is like

        a good war that

is an

idea

waged again
                                    may I
compare us to a sacrifice

            I shall

for good

        be groaning
   the conviction

withdraw so to project

   part touching

        y/our doorway

&

walk away

   the red stripe

is an opening

   on a growling joy

that's 'painterly'

           that's hanging from the tree
           as imitation in the
                smokies

mine of series
   moon of solace

fruit of the tree |
fruit of the floor | the seeds
shuddering on the floor |

we break my darling
but

&

in lying down

again to offer god

an image of my death

as styled against

the thought   (*this heap*

sneezing in my mask   *god bless you*

I am one / more saned / against

the doing of
          the digging out the bad part
of the nectarine
          that's bad
throughout

tonight I spoon against my wife
and say inside

   I've let the vehemence
and taken on the great coat   @ repose

&

said something

sounded like an insult ~~then~~ but wasn't then

"the calculus is changing"

which was

black block postcard

into the vanity

of record   &thisother(all is vanity

squirrel   book deposit   conversation w/

wife about the dow   all flows

yet the sea not full)

this passing   always to early

historyxx et   fall

consolation of philosophy

no consolation   no philosophy

what is at the bottom of

the glass   the glass

two

better than

one

&

maybe I can disappear into

the tax

    taxed packing
into this next

good faith

        signed in

        twin poles
of sleepy lights

that in the light

   this vapor of me

looks
full

but on the other side of me
      safe passage

&

frost flecks in the median or
        flakes of glass

it depends

        if eyes are on

spreading   sun
    of my day in the sun

with the dodge tool
        that my goods translucent
        lies over the ocean

my goods transparent
        is as much as
mine (what I call me)

as barrel stave
and tight cooperage

we walk   by

      the tourist crap

       husktacean

this was once

was preserve

we glare across the jetski dock
fish sandwich   tingling sea

@ the sound houses

     ~~there~~ built their

new no place

     towards the sound submerged

and the say change

&

the traitor in the chamber
gets opened up
as treason   is most inward

inward   is most treasonous
    dictators   dictators

        getting out all the banners
        from the side

as cloaks on cloaks

the stations of the clock

                        the bag of clocks
        my dear, please drop

                        (the wardrobe from the left side)

… proclaims me empty of

in the king's road
surrounded by the neighborhood
    dogs

spittle in the corner of the mouth
        as sovereignty gives rest
        learning gives counsel

not seeking windows
      as darkly

history keeps coming on the cusp
        all I may say / see

from this part of the tower   I am kept

tolerable well in this part

(we murder only breathing
           our way arbored)

the avenue of mansions
in the jetstream

&

come in   come in

no, ~~come in~~ incoming know

this hall is always open

        tunnel in
        tunnel out

to stick here in the thoroughfare
   porous prison of our limbs

~~break down the door~~
       patience as the deadbolts
      spring

  clockwork policy turn soft
      to answer

calling saints and angels
      all sloughing down

this highway
        in your mercy

    o honey

alls my pretty one

with this frontage always on
suspicion

&

in this period

it takes / work / to be / a self

       the sound

of what comes rushing

around the ears
      not it. . .

     before the television
     letting steam
         not

but   (care of)   ~~guy wire~~
  ~~pulley~~   jewel encrusted net

"talk"   agony of self by self

of being seen

        in the corner of the yard
        by the hollow trunk
        you'd fit in

    not that scene

but the body of the civic soul

        to be a self   in the street

hustling
           dangerous and dreadful

                              requiring daily naps

&

my darling   for clearing the way
    how is the garden

                gotten to

for   getting

        this sleet

we come to the line of scrimmage

what moves

            in the world

what does move it

                    agent of our closest star

who fed
who turned away
who clothed
who scorned

                justice in this middle age
            (seeping in this "flesh of one"

sanguine settlement)

        is crucifying

graft/ the clover on the dogwood

      no works in vain
      for giving ground

somewayd persisting

her mouth in the rain

I'll trust these
vegetable pigments
of rest

eye this long lease

against destruction

&

a voice said:

      put Heraclitus   over

duck

drink

the horse's draft

I conquer by enduring

enduring conquest

I make   mine amends

   unravel

   in devouring

   this writ(h)ing host

   of worms

friendship's ministry

   of oration

and tyrannies of bounty

lies over

   broken on the rack

of waters

   for the fruit

       for the tree on the fruit

wine to the horses bridles

&

prison of care   good god of surveillance

it doesn't escape the blinds of my soul

that loaves are not appearing from the sea

still   (of the pulse is closeness and foul bone

picked clean)   the worrying flow of the surf

transporting the foot

                    from print to print

remove shoes and enter

II

HOSPITALITY

THE FIRST POEM OF JAN VANDERMEER

a florid sunsets   evenings a drifting
eyes   my michigan (camaro hood propped
up with a hockey stick) of netherlands

behave my city doorless   the sick hand
knocking   sprouting a sapling at swingeings
alone escaped descriptions (partial) (cropped)

to this effect: I got flo   I got flo

THE SECOND POEM OF JAN VANDERMEER

I'm making bread precipitation   break

the heat

      the town comes up in wrinkles   sun

    scrolls

there up and down (see thus)   take
                      eat

if you're hungry (say what; see this)

the light ignites itself

    reveals the signature of distance
the silhouette
    inside the trunk

THE THIRD POEM OF JAN VANDERMEER

I shave my face and launch a bottle rocket
I scrape the walk to lurch into the highway

My face so smooth like the subtle field of scales
As no one asks the threshold how the light works

Just saunter through and halleloo   complexion
Verscheydenheden   world's fair   the world is fair

And foul   it reaches for me reaching for it
Above the city's face the breath invisible

That's mine

                    with sun behind the cloud of meaning
Of sunny civil   gestures   conversations

Vrau fair *vrau* foul and the littered tabletop
To battlefield   a serpentine transaction

My taste of wisdom come
Through plasters painting hurts

This one's a little happy   good for her

THE FOURTH POEM OF JAN VANDERMEER

1 static   2 static   3 network color   so

real
as swimming for the seats

the dartle of

their eyes (sometimes my picture looks;

like any other picture * still shivering)

we let some back into the stream –

their cold humor –

as close as deep, unreasonable

sewn with air

for seeing more end less

so flows my lens   slow jelly with ice

THE FIFTH POEM OF JAN VANDERMEER

Outside the town on fire

My pension of her grief

As she's turning

All of the moments of grief

On the moment of grief –

The woman draped in the featherbed

Her passion of the dead sea

In the monument

Bride *for wither you go*

I try

My porcelain of her grief

This residue of air

We mistook

   the remnant

Or mistake of sentiment

THE SIXTH POEM OF JAN VANDERMEER

As shook my darling's mind:

   foreign * forlorn * moraine
morse

(re)morse   as she was emptying

and emptying   specters in

traffic out front

of promising the world remains

   in the plash
« remainder »
        the road in thaw of
        paper foil as it's
        uncoming

THE SEVENTH POEM OF JAN VANDERMEER

The gusting snow in streetlight swarm of bees
Tonight to all the decaying mantles

Old wobbly world   tearing down   you make me hate me
You flinging light around your dark flung fill

Love comes up—my heart's late leach

Come work on me   come draw me out to work
For years are coming even absent ones

III

SONNETS MANQUÉS

#1

as was alleged the grizzled man goes months

Candide the thrift edition sits here dumb

it's empty time! they celebrate with crumbs

and pirate suites on pirate ships *en garde*

my pistol-grip *epée*   my devotion

I'm made of meat like them and do not change

but turn   the verso me the recto me

an opening   under the sun

in the breeze the turning world turns blowing

I know the rumor   birds pretend to sing

we hear the will   I say my prayers to them

the broke-wing crows   the winged imprimaturs

so heavy is your disappearing bar

#2

my father I dreamed you had hanged yourself

over algebra   which seemed odd   but as

the metaphors for x and y perhaps

your algebra is grave

and you know x the neighbor cat   got hit

one cat-long wound x turned upon itself

in the right lane   (take away x what's left)

the street that runs from Flint to Bowling Green

the time it takes to judge the world to death

$$x$$

where tracks are crossing bound for lakes of soot

the kid plays cigarettes   removes a rib

it *is* the afternoon   I didn't know

the rays of afternoon were underfoot

the task of taking on a skin like rose

we've tried to grow them   petal and stem

are skin like taking on a film of soot

Detroit   the city of roses and phlegm

what color   Jesus Detroit   what resolve

invisible except in light   the root

the disappearing wither weatherer

until the pulp comes through in fingerprint

I'm stunned into silence   only to sing

I am   the opening out   I accept

the work   to throw my voice

against the stripes and the strepitation

the belt of the assembler creeping on

to make the rose again in my climate

#4

is just greatness and marvel absolute

the kingdom where I'm listening to limbs:

my thirty dollar wheelbarrow   brims

with rainwater (mosquito eggs) the fruit

of empty space   of comets named for sands

prepare thy face   especially thy jaw

to bear it   striking kingdom on the star

from waving heat   absorbing angry hands

absorb the yard   the squalling crow and jay

hortus inconclusus with all that sky

above it   where generations have lived

(have rigged)   the lilac tree and bleeding heart

the broken lyric of my awe and dread

I pass and wait for blows and strength to wait

#5

The sign says

      CREW
        IN
      TREES

           the crew above

is sweeping angels nets with bowing hooks

each word is flavored says the synesthete:

CREW tastes of jackdaw   IN of crane   and TREES

of Saint Bernard   the rain begins to turn

their thoughts to rain   the embassy must fall

on island cane like snow   on inland rice

I hit the signal   swing left around them

for birdnest soup that tastes like OLD KINGDOM

in a can

#6

as the message "innocent as sunshine"

is what?   these geese?   in the high grass and dew

is visible today   is the highschool

as I'm imagining sunshine this time

as night   the star of david as a sun

isn't shining   *what happens after dark*

as in the depths   as with the angler fish

in the streetlight through the branches of gum

as innocence is a negative state

I "can but prophesy"   it won't be done

tomorrow   innocent as tomorrow

the saving turn that is as *from* the sun

into knowing whatnot   the high grass grows

as the horizon on the horizon

#7

For everything that's shrinking is a span

spoke   splayed on the ice @ one crazy glass

@ two black branches   stars put up again

to fall on alabama   falling past

one story after two   it breaks the bowl

of dirty water   sitting here to boil

in rainfall winds (turned corners) as they stir

the edges off the distillation's soul

that prison that I visit   history

destroying engine @ the latch   my rust

uncouples from stator from flux   exact

goodbye *exact*   thus swings the hinge   they fly

those atoms look like things and rise and act

this breathing out across the tiles in dust

#8

if what this means could be protected from

Serrano could protect me from the range

the rain (quite beautiful) into the sink

incessant pool of body in the self

shit, man   man shits on man   it's common sense

I'm built around an anus   less in sum

than parts   o part of me that breaks for change

and a cup of coffee   no "span"   that's life

so pissing on it stripes the god that dies

endures the span that's life   it reenacts

the myth of living   living   excrement

so "nothing's shocking"   jesus streams in sees

peculiar washing   couth unstrange   ascent /

decline / ascent that's life   expand contract

54

#11

O, bellbottoms in the snow   dragging damp

To kick off roemers   light through fresh peeled fruit

Across the scurvy coat (dirtied with soot)

Shit winter passing through the shorting lamp

reflexyconst
like   likenesses
in   visages   in
escape routes

I'm studying the canvas weave for holes

And finding study cooked in sacks of raw

Oysters shining on the platter   patches

I've looked for on a big counter   doses

Then happy genre then the good auld saw:

"if you know music without notes, play that"

IV

FROM THE
RESTORATION

little ward

        [my urchin spirit]

[:: which is the] Fonder choice sun? shade?
Awe? Ache?

[if Adept Lu chooses one, how can the other be wrong?]

My task
Work

[,or charge,]

        li t t
                  le

                        ease [::]

To the space I was   am now   in

in a column [my narrative excuse]

bred in Fetters under
the labor
under

[the rail between the stiles]

[::] f all

      fault

          my self

[straight is the gate / narrow the way /

        my narrative extends to include origins over the lip
             of history]

[::] above my reach

the prime work

dark *ami* of noon [my mother and father of birds—but also vultures]

        Soul such a tender eye [socket ward]

A moving captivity

The sphear of

      The Earth

[::] joy

counsel   console

Friends   revive

     by talk

         friends

[all]
      Roads [lead to the door of the domicile]

warm
          Friends

[in the deep cottage in the wickedness]

any   sound

chases   ease

linde [n]

   o a k

rusted to

the

woman   Friends

minted

      days

[::]   in   domos   paird

      These two portions

[boundless]

pri[z]es

      beside

The Nation

 The

intimate impulse

[::] I might begin

 roving

(o I never

was

The   Monster   [see: my narrative of meekness]

      share

[I] gave my [shelter] to a woman

Rising   just to

The cords; threads [r&b shop]

      The Towers

deserts [who condensed to fill the whole shop like smoke]

[::] there may be who think not God at all,
       they walk obscure

in

another   inward
uncouth   place
      here

where

Angels walk'd
in trust

In mortal strength!   in man
     and thing

       are gifts desirable [?]

[if Adept Kung wears silk, how can it be wrong? I don't know if it is desirable.]

[::] [cosy in] our rest hive

   [cosily] thrust into a Dungeon [of comfort]   to work

at

deeds

   for sake of deeds

      [that] seek repose and rest

I yield and unlock all

[::] Marriage

state

    and

Temptation

    the burden of trust

This Feast
and Sacrifice

agon
Beside

    Wine

in   the   house

our

agon   dances

around

blear

harbour

This only hope relieves me, that strife
Is   anothe[r]   name
Fo[r]
Worship

in   this   light

elected / pains and slaveries

[::] I deserve spare punishment

friend

as a blab

But [admire]

Gentle Parables

perhaps [perhaps]
God will relent

[:: if Yu remembers his mother and father, who can say he is wrong?]

Reject not

who knows / But God hath set before us

[in] this house

voluptuous life [as a way]

[::] tame Weather
turn me out [read back: my pieties are suspect]

Desire of   all delicious

stream[s   consumes me]

I drank

      that turbulent liquor / madness

[I learned]

      temperance /// can be useful

and work on the household hearth

[can be] droning

[I] drudge [bee]   earn // Consume

[and work to] welcom all

[::] at home lie [if Yen Hui lies at home, where will he not lie?]

       genial spirits

            within

       [read back: my] mind   humours
         fancy

               friends

[my fancies breed ill humors and the]
   bodies wounds and sores

In

  th'inmost mind

the

           tenderest parts

  in the list of them that hope

         [they are also in my mind]
           a tune

       within

wandering loose about

[::] safety

                         come near
she moves

                her

         feet and

                         tears [the rice paper skin of rest]

    with amends

[::] To

                 submit, beseech
And reconcile

Confess and promise

                 to try

[::]   to reject

to / draw to

my

weakness

In me

safety

i   s [a kind of]

weakness

[weakness] of kind

gentle[,]   severely / dear /   tuning

safety:

in   safe custody

at home   full of   fears

[::] in

Here   day and night

            home of partners

                            well meaning

[if]
    compassion

                                                    displays

            malice

                            [what does no compassion display?]

[::]   Love seeks to

                            cover

Or   uncover

            Snares [as for snares, I don't know if they are bad or good]

[::]   in person [now at my door,
the road whizzing with devils and saints in transit of agonies and hopes]

[::]   to the public good [*Jen*]/ Private respects must yield /
full possession

[::] enemies

receive me

under their protection [I render them tribute ... rest in their bosom]

mine,   theirs

[']I was worried
I was a fool

Forgive / me[']

[::] At home

in

this loathsom prison-house   abide
With me
nurs   e   me

No, no,   no

no

No [let me nurse you]

my feet
have been caught

in most things [not least of which doors]

This Gaol I count the house of Liberty
        whose doors my feet

enter /// joint by joint

[::] claims   deeds

   s   ing   h   er

      name

In   the border

              [in the plaster, masonry, pine floor, and basement mold]

  in my countrey where I most desire

      hospitable

 secresie,   safety, and   life

  secret sting

       in   concord

  it is hard [not to fear the end of concord]

[::] too much
     root [the privets here were never pruned

    they've stifled themselves at last like]

contrar[i]es

[::] cleaving
            turbulence

Draws him [the humane]

To

That
Happy   house!   peace is smooth:
But vertue   breaks the

        h   ost [into sacramental food]

[::]   Or peace or not

arrives

Hath walk'd about / The way to

know were not to see but taste

in the house   [but]

the

Marriage [made it riddle clear: stay put, feed others]

[::] Some narrow place enclos'd   [perspective box where] sight
Or rather flight
                  [reminds of soul]
        thy gorgeous arms

with-hold me

Again in safety

glorious arms

Thir ornament and safety

whose God is strongest // In the common prison

no
locks

[::]   our   word

                                                is
                                        subdu'd
                        in
knowledge [excuse my narrative]

                                god is God

        a Robber   rob s

                friends   guests

    ring

My Nation

                force with force [and what can be the yield but force?]

I [say labor not force   even I] a private person

Single

        private   person

[better to be]   fetter'd [thus], but   free

[::] This

bulk
                    is

hazard / ou s

            [I've historicized it ... it isn't clay]

[::]
            vulg a r

   e l ect / ion

m   or   e   afflict // ion

            plain enough
Much more affliction

The work of   hands

   ,

Is   not

   patient

[::]

   tyrannie

       of

  Patience
This Idol day hath bin   no day of rest
   Labouring
        working

      tending

    the

        Publick Mill // My self my conscience and internal peace

[come in   take out   the surplus flour]

      my strength

labour

power

are

hamper / e   d

I could be   content

I am content

To

be   nothing [but surplus flower]

[::] dread once   now [quiet]

God   Law   Nation   self

at home

[semi-]Private reward

[to] dread

to live   poor
        in that   prison

is

                        to forgo [living]

            wanting   I shall want nothing [but what I want]

It shall be my delight to tend

            in the house

t o

d   o

service

Not to sit idle with so great a gift

[::]

       The first-born bloom of spring
Nipt with the lagging rear of winters frost

[will they come   *'and I remember one of them said: we do not pray for*
a great harvest   *we pray for the strength to bring it in'* will I welcome
them]

  glorious hand

The Edifice where all

                  enter

                        spectacle [of (some say) salvation]

                with mirth, high chear, & wine

  the   roof

The whole roof

this Feast

The vulgar who stood without [latinate modifiers]

in

necessity [deferred to in casuistry]

welcomed   jocund   sublime
                        internal

    inward   illuminated

                        perch

    nest

Of

                        Wood

        of

clotted gore

      my kindred   my friends
                     attend

Home

      plant it round with

           Acts
     or sweet Lyric Song

           though we oft doubt

    th'unsearchable

[though maybe a 'pious wish': salvation the way   *T'ien*]

  peace and consolation / calm of mind

V

PENALTY

LETTER FROM PRISON

He sinks to the foot of the water trap

where all spires start   *umbilicus mundi*

the bath descends   the lathe   the lap

and fanning rain

as it is remedied before or so

to keep his footing

The black consortium of lift   of drag

in his head the Athenaeum

tapped from concertina

"I will relent"

   and unafraid

or "take me, make haste"

PRISONER'S WREATH

From this step I may beckon as from home
Home from the spinning yardsale spooled nowhere
Nowhere spooled in nothing   except the groan
Which is a song   of no sale   of no care
Care for me in all my ways   of bondage
Bond me to this makeshift house   shifting walls
Walled up this stuff   I stuff into my stash
Stash my stuff with simple care until full
Filled with work and stuff the day disappears
Invisible church   Invisible stone
The stone walk uneven   boxwood not pared
Pair nothing   don't strain   never be alone

REUBEN'S FEAR, SIMEON'S SORROW, LEVI'S HOPE, & JUDAH'S LOVE

It sticks with us   with us it sticks
That climbing we should   should we climb
Be limed or lured to springes
I'm lousy
        With sticks and grass-stain bedhead

I ... strive to prove / The constancy and virtue
of your Love   but striving sticks here:
like fireworks my works   my works like fireworks
I call the stars a token and shovel the snow

Nice and syllogistic   fell and melancholy given
The effort concocted right escapes to "things
indifferent"   I owe it to my neighbors

Care   do
        but too much care is different

                                it's fear and sorrow

This sticks with us   I fear my neighbors
All the same I wish them well

LETTER FROM PRISON

us with no light

the dog edging its nose

out the window and snapping the air

for a beacon   the river turned over

the congregation   stretched

Paul says   I, therefore,

prisoner of the Lord

on interstates stay

on interstates

sputtering little generator in the neighborhood

just work worthy

for emergency spills   in my unbelief

more frequent since

the testimony

PRISONER'S WREATH

This charcoal way surrounds my spot in dust
Dusty property   the grit of the word
Word it so the song persists in a trust
The trust you've shown with hardness in the void
The plenum: I   The window's open now
Now open the circumcision for air
Air out the room with that mouth on this vowel
Umbilicus mundi here   room to spare
Spare us in your mercy from too close air
My eyes are closed   I wait for guests disguised
Disguised guests may come and go at leisure
Leisure here at my expense   try this leisure

THERE IT HURTS ME

There where the yellow spot is   the finger
Points

There it hurts me

In the hovering house

The form of that thing I've fallen in

Or illusions of my doubt

*

Legs in the breach

Gently pressing at the perimeter

Between the greeting and the granting of audience

The yellow spot   lines converging
At the mark on the door

The confession you are looking for

I have it here

LETTER FROM PRISON

OK to the reservoir

as far as from the rock

to the shovel

the gaze of these strange birds

on this blue bowl I broke

with a flail

this bowl I loved

my drawing sentiments

seen   before

in the proverb

all is vanity

drawing the bath

bathing the sight in

cold humors

til freedom or perfect regulation

as the many styles of death

present

    as many darlings as

PRISONER'S WREATH

As storm drains cull / collect the leafy curb
Curb the horse the dog the song the mountain
Mountain of my youth   what can you   absorb. . .
Absorb the string   the calculus rhythm
Arrhythmias of stream leave gritty wash
And wash the bed and empty set the pail
Pale proportion close cinder block: I'm crushed
Crushed on these phenomena of the light
Things swimming in light   we dust motes of style
Style us in curbs outside waters inside

ADAM NAMING THE DISEASES

for Michael Schoenfeldt

from the mountain between jerusalem
I see them   kreutsfeldt   jakob   lou gehrig
before [my] *eyes sad noysom dark*   in which
the bandage "reeks"   the landscape has no term*

there is no time   deluge of biting flies
ezek'l in the valley cries the hand
*determination   frenzy   no   demand
in living   death   in dying living lies

the name   the signature that dies   is both
clinic window   clinic cage   ("pathologos")

the wet within the dark   THAT LIVES FOR LIGHT
bacterial infection   (also, "life")

the double adam   (panacea)   (bane)
the ransom cultures   stands above the name

LETTER FROM PRISON

which one of these:

galactic wrap

        make dinner
        wash up

atomic fizz

        vacuum this
        scrub at that

or running along the fencerow

with your stick

in the freedoms of noise on noise

it's sometimes sweltering

even when it looks to wind itself

a corkscrew

in here

my collaborator

some days I wake to confusion

you and I, our precedents

where the windows are
where the bars

PRISONER'S WREATH

Insatiable cormorant come light by me
By me you feast on black and white and cry
Mule more than cry good stubborn bird of seals
Seals of consequence these red cracker crumbs
Crumbling on vertices and horizons
Orisons notwithstanding too late now
Now is the greeting of the pelicans
Feeding their blood to their infinite young
We are friends aren't we and young and fed there
At their threshold just damp with the change
(The colliquating penance of the cracks)
Cracks gone in mercies and skeins on wet wings

LETTER FROM PRISON

the will to open

with corrosion

the bear claw genre

if they were turned away

waved along   lighted by a soda burn

it avails not

the distance (the grammar of your variety)

of my grief at it

all the air above me

though welcome to their gaze

goes humid

down to forces *forces*

PRISONER'S WREATH

To tell instead   it is a foreign song
Before the interstate   we must reform
Reform me by several means and gray ways
Ways in and out   I have   this government
Government of fouls and burning bitters
I bite a hole in orange to open
Reform the us a little   but here first
This room I've prepared   I can't make it out
Out of dirt from dust from the patient tense
Penitent stretched   in compass of a pale

CONFESSION

in how we walk
we essay on
our own good fortune
the millipede of merit

thus are designed the sarcophagi
   intact on top
   all toady below

as we walk

we undertake one way

our way   gridded and girded
with other ways

we may take
but don't or don't know we're taking

this way

to the muffled report
of all these pigeons
starting right then cutting left
like swarms of bog flies

outside and inside the physical heart

ABOUT THE AUTHOR

Aaron McCollough has published two previous collections of poetry, *Welkin* (Ahsahta Press, 2002) and *Double Venus* (Salt, 2003). He and Suzanne Chapman have been living in Ann Arbor, Michigan, with their schnauzer, Gertrude.

Ahsahta Press

SAWTOOTH POETRY PRIZE SERIES

2002: Aaron McCollough, *Welkin* (Brenda Hillman, judge)

2003: Graham Foust, *Leave the Room to Itself* (Joe Wenderoth, judge)

2004: Noah Eli Gordon, *The Area of Sound Called the Subtone* (Claudia Rankine, judge)

2005: Karla Kelsey, *Knowledge, Forms, The Aviary* (Carolyn Forché, judge)

NEW SERIES

1. Lance Phillips, *Corpus Socius*

2. Heather Sellers, *Drinking Girls and Their Dresses*

3. Lisa Fishman, *Dear, Read*

4. Peggy Hamilton, *Forbidden City*

5. Dan Beachy-Quick, *Spell*

6. Liz Waldner, *Saving the Appearances*

7. Charles O. Hartman, *Island*

8. Lance Phillips, *Cur aliquid vidi*

9. Sandra Miller, *Oriflamme*

10. Brigitte Byrd, *Fence Above the Sea*

11. Ethan Paquin, *The Violence*

12. Ed Allen, *67 Mixed Messages*

13. Brian Henry, *Quarantine*

14. Kate Greenstreet, *case sensitive*

15. Aaron McCollough, *Little Ease*

Ahsahta Press

MODERN AND CONTEMPORARY POETRY OF THE AMERICAN WEST

This book is set in Apollo MT type with Perpetua Titling MT titles
by Ahsahta Press at Boise State University
and manufactured on acid-free paper
by Boise State University Printing and Graphics, Boise, Idaho.
Cover design by Quemadura.
Book design by Janet Holmes.

AHSAHTA PRESS
2006

JANET HOLMES, DIRECTOR
CHRISTOPHER JAMES KLINGBEIL
ERIK LEAVITT
JANNA VEGA
ALLISON VON MAUR
ABIGAIL L. WOLFORD